BRITAIN IN OLD PHOTOGRAPHS

AROUND DURHAM

MICHAEL RICHARDSON

Billy Longstaff, enjoying a smoke on his pipe, sitting at his kitchen range at 32 The Crescent, Sherburn Village, 1974. He was an ex-miner, model engineer and keen amateur photographer. This photograph was taken by Ray Kitching.

SUTTON PUBLISHING LIMITED

Sutton Publishing Limited
Phoenix Mill · Thrupp · Stroud
Gloucestershire · GL5 2BU

First published 1998

Copyright © Michael Richardson, 1998

British Library Cataloguing in Publication Data
A catalogue record for this book is available from the
British Library.

ISBN 0-7509-2073-4

Typeset in 10/12 Perpetua.
Typesetting and origination by
Sutton Publishing Limited.
Printed in Great Britain by
Ebenezer Baylis, Worcester.

To
Emma and Michelle

Edward Button (author's great-great-uncle),
1880s, wearing the uniform of the 4th
Volunteer Battalion Durham Light Infantry. A
platelayer by trade, he lived at Belmont station.
After spending New Year's Eve, 31 December
1903, at Sunderland he took a train to
Leamside station. There he waited for a goods
train to pass so that he could jump on it for a
lift. He was found in the early evening at the
side of the line between Leamside and Belmont
station after falling from a wagon. He died from
his injuries a week later in the County Hospital.

CONTENTS

George March, porter/signalman, Pittington station, photographed by D. Jaques of Gateshead, *c.* 1910. He is wearing the corduroy uniform of the North Eastern Railway. George, who retired in the 1950s, was from High Pittington. He was the uncle of Ray Kitching, railway enthusiast and photographer.

INTRODUCTION

The cover picture of this, the fifth collection of old photographs of the Durham area collected by Michael Richardson to be published by Sutton Publishing, shows the milkmaids of Houghall and serves as a reminder that rural pursuits have long existed even within the boundaries of Durham City. But, as Norman Emery has commented in his *The Coal Miners of Durham* (Sutton Publishing, 1992), in County Durham 'coal was king'. The villages depicted in this book, all now within the extended boundaries of the city, all lying east of the old city, were all dependent upon the coal industry and all formed part of the great East Durham coalfield. Coal was mined in County Durham from the twelfth century to the early 1990s, but in the last thirty years the decline has been such that a whole traditional way of life has been transformed; the Miners' Gala on the second Saturday in July has been reduced to a shadow of its former self and Durham mining now means open-cast coal extraction mostly in the west of the county. The evidence for a great industry which underpinned Britain's economy in the nineteenth and early twentieth centuries is now largely to be found in the landscape, in the memories of older people and in memories of such characters as George Parkinson (commemorated in the Sherburn Aged Miners' Homes, illustrated here) who records in his *True Stories of Durham Pit Life* (1912) that he went down the pit in New Lambton at the age of nine in 1837. In the words of Bill Dowding, 'The Pit Road' (1993):

> Only the ash remains of older pits in elephantine capes
> Only the ash remains, once recognised and loved in human form
> The dead face emptied of its life and worth
> Only the ash remains in mother earth.

To my mind, the great contribution made by such old photographs as are here gathered together is the record they constitute of things long past and soon likely to be forgotten without trace if this visual evidence did not receive publicity. The highly significant Grange Iron works at Carrville, recorded here in several photographs, was formerly engaged in a massive export trade, but closed in 1926 and was bombed during the last war; it is now a caravan site and its name lingers in that of a public house. County Durham has very few traces of Tudor times and it is good to be reminded of the Elizabethan origins of Elemore Hall near Pittington. Rebuilt in the eighteenth century, it was the centre of a large estate and is now a residential school run by Durham County Council. The manor house at Ludworth, represented in the collection by a photograph of the Tower, had the most southerly of pele towers but is now a ruin in the care of the City Council. Sherburn Hall shown here, which had been owned by such noted families as the Tempests, Hoppers, Thompsons and Coulsons was demolished in the 1950s. Houghall Manor, of which there is a rare 1930s view, went in the 1960s and Cross Street, Houghall, a group of miners' cottages, is now a few foundations on the Houghall Nature Trail.

Michael Richardson has always taken a particular interest in photographs portraying people. Three photographs I found of special interest. There is a picture of William Simpson of Littletown, a miner and well-known bonesetter of the 1870s who rode his horse wearing a distinctive top hat and swallow-tailed coat. Miners have always been given to growing leeks and there is a photograph of leek show attenders in 1958 enjoying a pan of prize leek broth made by the landlady of the Londonderry Arms, Sherburn Hill. Another portrait is of the great character, whom I knew personally, J. Wesley Lisle, the deaf and dumb shoe and boot repairer of Church Street who carried on his business from 1927 to his death in 1977 with an absolutely fabulous sense of humour.

Much more could be written about these unique pictures of Durham's past, but it is for the reader to relish at leisure whatever takes the fancy the most.

Professor G.R. Batho
Durham 1998

Durham County Council members viewing a model for the proposed new County Hall, February 1958. Left to right: Mr G.R. Clayton, County Architect, Coun. J. Coxon, Chairman of the County Council, Coun. J.S. Goodwin, Mr J.K. Hope, Clerk to the Council, Alderman R. Shotton, Chairman of the Finance Committee, Alderman J.A. Robinson, Chairman of the Education Committee and Coun. W. Beck. The new building, begun in 1960, was officially opened by His Royal Highness Prince Philip, Duke of Edinburgh on 14 October 1963.

CHAPTER ONE

DURHAM CITY

Looking down Framwellgate, Durham (which was once part of the Great North Road), from the junction at the bottom of Castle Chare, c. 1933. The fine venetian window and coach entrance, seen on the left, are a reminder of the more elegant properties that once stood in this area. They were demolished as part of the slum clearance in the early 1930s.

An aerial view of Gilesgate, Durham, showing the 'duck pond' area, late 1950s. The actual duck pond was approximately where the flower-bed is now, on the south side of the green. Near it (bottom left) are Wood & Watson's, mineral water manufacturers, and the Gilesgate Nursery School (closed in about 1981). The former factory site is now being developed by Cussins Homes. St Giles' church can be seen, top right.

John Metcalfe (right), cartwright and undertaker, outside his premises, 106 Gilesgate (now owned by Durham Veterinary Group), c. 1924. The business had been started by his uncle, John Blenkinsop, cartwright and joiner, in about 1836. When the nephew took over he added undertaking also; he retired in the early 1970s. Thurkettle's butcher's van from Gilesgate Moor is seen after being repaired.

The Canteen Inn, 97 Gilesgate, now a private house, *c.* 1916. The landlord, John R. Beeby, wearing the waistcoat, became landlord of the Bay Horse (now the Durham Light Infantryman) in November 1917. On the right was the old Gilesgate Methodist Church, now an undertakers.

The Gilesgate Moor Inn, Marshall Terrace, Gilesgate Moor, on the corner of Marshall Terrace and Belle Vue Terrace, opposite the Grange Foundry public house, *c.* 1900. Mrs E. Shaw, who ran it, is on the left. It is now retail premises: a hardware and DIY shop, with a hairdresser above.

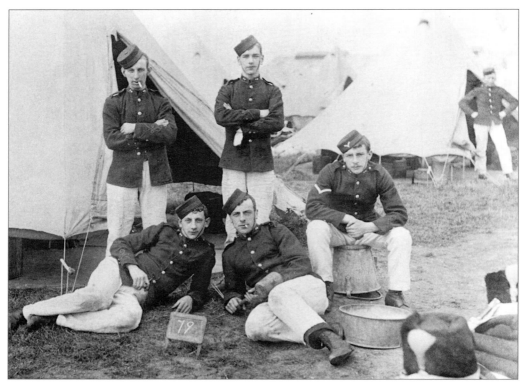

Soldiers from the 2nd Durham Artillery Volunteers at annual camp, *c.* 1906. Standing in the centre is Richard A. Addison of Saddler Street.

The band of the 8th Durham Light Infantry at the bottom of Gilesgate bank marching towards Claypath, seen here passing through lower Gilesgate, *c.* 1908. The Woodman Inn is to the rear of the group on the left.

The Sunderland Echo office, 24 Market Place, 1947. Standing outside the window are, left to right, George Harris, office manager, Joseph March, junior clerk, and Herbert Wilson, reporter. Above can be seen the office of Freeman & Son Ltd, solicitors. The shop on the left is Duoro Wine Shops Ltd.

Boots Chemists, 29 Silver Street, 1947. The premises are now The Works bookshop and stationers. Left to right: Elsie Chapman, Jean Appleby, Doris Young, Rita Bland, Marion Batey and Laura Milne.

Staff from The Provincial Laundries Ltd, The Sands, *c.* 1927. Second from the left is William Dixon Slack (see page 34). Part of the building was later used as the GPO parcel office before this moved to new premises on the Belmont Industrial Estate.

Staff from Nelson's Harness and Saddle Makers, 21 Market Place, 1910. Back row, second left, is Frederick Louis Adamson (a freeman of the city). In the centre of the front row is the works' cat! John Nelson ran the concern with his brother Thomas. John had taken over this long-established business from Thomas Scawin for whom he had worked.

Alex Gleason, tinsmith, 3 South Street, late 1930s. The sign in the window reads, 'Pram Wheels Re-tyred'. The shop stood to the right of the Fighting Cocks public house.

Benjamin Gleason, tinsmith, 55 New Elvet, 1920s. The skills of the tinplate worker have now vanished. This shop stood next to the old Hare and Hounds on the site (approximately) of the open space between Dunelm House and Elvet Riverside.

Mr J. Wesley Lisle, shoe and boot repairer, The Bungalows, Palmers Close, Church Street, *c.* 1931. Mr Lisle established the business in 1927 and continued up until his death on 12 January 1977. The sign in the window reads 'Gents, Soled & Heeled 4/9d, Ladies 2/9d'. The shed and contents were saved and are now at Beamish Museum.

A cart decorated for the Durham City Horse Parade, from Fentiman's Botanical Brewers, of The Hallgarth, showing Edith and Arthur Fentiman, *c.* 1913. The building in the background is part of the old tithe barn, now Durham Prison Officers' Club. Fentiman's ginger beer has recently been produced again by a member of the Fentiman family.

Clarke's Library Book Co., 28 New Elvet, c. 1931. Left to right: Karl Adamson (later to marry Jane Slack), -?- , Mrs E. Clarke, Jane Dixon Slack. The business later moved to North Road. This shop is now a branch of Lloyds Bank.

A water-colour of Salvin's Woollen Mill, Church Street, due south of St Oswald's Church. There were 8 floors and 365 windows. The picture, dated 1846 and signed 'M. Thompson', must have been drawn from memory, as a fire destroyed the mill on 6 January 1804. It had been operating for only eight years. Part of its north wall survives as a boundary wall to the churchyard.

A 1919 United bus, *c.* 1921. United began its life as a public transport operator in Lowestoft on 4 April 1912; later that year a second service was running between Bishop Auckland and Durham.

A United bus photographed near the New Inn, Church Street, 1920s. Note the solid tyres which must have given passengers quite a rough ride on Durham's cobbled streets. The advertisement at the rear of the bus is for Heinz spaghetti. The western towers of the cathedral can be seen on the right.

The High Sheriff, the Hon. James Arthur Joicey, reading the proclamation of the accession of King George V from the steps of the County Court House, Old Elvet, 11 May 1910. He is wearing the full dress uniform of the Northumberland Fusiliers. He had arrived exactly at noon in the state coach drawn by four bays, with footmen and trumpeters in attendance. The photograph was taken by Wilkinson.

Councillor Tom Sharp, left, landlord of the Lord Seaham Inn (Sharp Crescent, Gilesgate Moor, was named after him), seen with Tom Pierrepoint, the hangman, who lodged in the Lord Seaham (now Gilesgate Moor Hotel) when in Durham on business. The photograph was taken by Ernest, 21 Silver Street, in the late 1930s. Tom Pierrepoint worked with his brother Henry and was later joined by his nephew Albert, who resigned in 1956.

Adams' confectioners shop, 14 Claypath, Sunday 24 April 1949. The queue was due to the de-rationing of sweets – the first to come off rations in seven years. In the centre is Norman Richardson's first travel agent's shop; on the right is the Wearmouth Bridge public house.

Adams' shop, 21 Silver Street, showing on the left the steps leading to the riverside walk, with another de-rationing queue, 24 April 1949. Above the shop was Holdsworth's photographer's studio. The site is now occupied by a 1960s building, which contains offices and a pizza restaurant.

Samuel Adams & Co., manufacturing confectioners, Dee Cee Works, New Elvet, floodlit at the end of the war and viewed from across the river, May 1945. In March 1940 a fire destroyed a large part of the old factory. This photograph shows the new factory building at night, and was taken by Daisy Edis.

Carnival parade for the coronation of King George VI, May 1937. The decorated float belonged to the City Corporation. On it are St Margaret's junior boys wearing the actual shirts worn by Sunderland football team, the cup-winners against Preston at Wembley on 3 May. Back row, left to right: -?-, Jim Marsden, Harry Lawson, -?-, Alan Nelson, Frank Fletcher. Front row: Arthur Lawson, Freddie Holland, -?-, Ted Nelson, Bill Steadman. Standing: (?) Mr George Forman, Mr Arthur Coxon, Mr F. Holland, Mr J. Marsden.

Durham City Association Football Club, 1920/1, Top row, left to right: Barnes, Patchett, J. Sowerby (sec.), T. Holliday (chairman), T. Turner (treasurer), Redpath, Dobson. Middle row: Vincent, Avery, Davison, Cowell. Bottom row: Ferguson, Toward, Cousins, Young, Heather, Pattison, Thompson.

Durham City Football Club in Barcelona during their Spanish tour, 1924. Many faces can be matched with the photograph above. This photograph was taken by Foto-Sport, Madrid. Durham Football Association was formed on 25 May 1883 in the Three Tuns Hotel, New Elvet. It was not until 1918 that an attempt was made to form a Durham City Club.

CHAPTER TWO

BELMONT & BROOMSIDE

Interior of St Mary Magdalene, Belmont, 1920s. The church was consecrated on 15 October 1857 and the architect was William Butterfield. Minor alterations were carried out in 1872, the north porch was added in 1889 and the vestry in 1901. The Revd J.B.J. Bevan is standing in the nave. The church has recently suffered from the trend of re-ordering, one victim being the old font, which has been buried in the churchyard.

Belmont church and schools, *c.* 1910. The road to the right leads to Broomside Lane. The first school, which opened in 1838 before the church was built, can be seen behind the trees in the old churchyard. On the right are the old 1870 school buildings (see below).

Belmont school, *c.* 1920. It was designed by Austin & Johnson in 1870 and has now been converted into private residences, appropriately named The Old School House and The Old School.

Teachers from Belmont school, Broomside Lane, c. 1923. The Headmaster, Thomas E. Venner (seated) was appointed Head on 1 January 1915, with a salary of £145 per annum.

A class from Belmont school, 1915. Many of the children were from families connected with either the iron works or the local collieries.

Looking towards Durham from the junction of Belmont and Carrville showing, on the right, the Sportsman's Arms (see below), 1920s. A bus can be seen travelling towards Durham via Gilesgate Moor.

The Sportsman's Arms Inn, Moor Edge, Carrville, *c.* 1910. The landlord Mr Robert McCutcheon is in the centre wearing a waistcoat.

The Red Triangle Hut, Belmont, officially opened by Queen Victoria's granddaughter, Princess Marie Louise, who is seen holding the bouquet, 26 October 1921. Next to her is Dean Welldon. She had just opened a Young Men's Christian Association fête in Durham Town Hall during her visit to the north-east. Afterwards, on her way to Sunderland, she and her party were received by Mr H.P. Hayle, agent at the Grange Iron Works and president of the Belmont Hut (which had been open for twenty months). The club was lost when the Carrville section of the A1(M) was built in the 1960s.

Belmont Cricket Team, c. 1953. Back row, left to right: S. Martin, R. Sutherland, M. Kirby, W. Portway, E. Thompson, R. Maughan, L. Cooke, R. Hudspith, R. Martin, W. Tiplady. Middle row: W. Cummings (umpire), B. Robinson, F. Bruce, L. Martin, L. Griggs, N. Martin (capt.), R. Cole, S. Birtie, A. Tulip, J. Robinson, R. Martin, Mr Hodgkiss (umpire). Front row: Mr Thompson, -?-, Mr Tiplady, Mr Turnbull, -?-, Mr Lowe, -?-, Mr Thompson, Mr Cummings, -?-, Mr C. Booth. Seated: P. Brown and E. Wright.

1st Belmont Scout Troop (founded 1919), outside the church porch, August 1925. Back row, left to right: Cockrill, L. Hope, J. Wilkinson, W. Watson, L. Parnaby, Lofthouse, Wright. Middle row: W. Lambeth, W. Gray, Fred Gray, the Revd J.B.J. Bevan, R. Appleby, R. Gray, N. Edgar. Front row: W. Cummings, M. Curren, Clough, Coulson, L. Hind.

Belmont Association Football Team, 1950s. Back row, left to right: B. Nichol, J. Hill, E. Wright, A. Dunhill, S. Sweet, T. Thompson, J. Walton, A. Bertram, N. Thompson, R. Curry. Front row: T. Shingler, A. Piper, K. Greenwood, G. Marley, F. Crago, D. Clough, C. Ashworth. In front: T. Thompson, jnr.

Broomside Colliery (Lady Adelaide Pit), drawn by T.H. Hair and etched by J. Brown, *c.* 1840. The colliery, sunk in 1829, closed in 1889. Broomside is described in Kelly's Directory (1921) as a colliery village belonging to Belmont, chiefly inhabited by pitmen and workers at the Grange Iron Works.

The bar of the Londonderry Inn, Broomside Lane, which stood at the corner of Bainbridge Street and Broomside Lane, *c.* 1920. It is believed to show George Gray and his family who ran the pub from 1900 to 1922. Very few photographs exist of interior views of Durham public houses.

The old Travellers' Rest, Broomside Lane, showing the landlord, Robert Bowman (without hat to the right of the door), *c.* 1910. The present Travellers' Rest was built on a new site nearby in the 1960s.

Mr Albert Hill, known as 'Albert the Black', centre front, an American who was brought to England as a professional runner, *c.* 1918. He made Broomside his home after his racing days had finished and became a miner. The photograph was taken outside the Working Men's Club, which had previously been the old Mason's Arms (closed 23 December 1909), Broomside Lane. It is now a double-fronted private house, opposite The Links.

CHAPTER THREE

CARRVILLE

Thomas (Sunny) Hardy, coal dealer, Carrville, early 1930s. He is sitting in his 1930 Ford Model AA lorry. Sunny was born in Carrville and worked all his life as a coal merchant and haulage contractor. The business has been continued by his son and grandson.

Looking down Carrville High Street, c. 1910. Kelly's Directory of 1921 describes Carrville as a village in the parish of Belmont consisting chiefly of one street.

Looking up Carrville towards Durham, c. 1920. On the right is the King's Arms. In the 1930s the attic rooms of the houses were heightened to make an extra floor. The pebble-dashed and rendered fronts disguise this alteration. All but no. 43 were altered.

The first Carrville branch of the Pittington Co-op, *c.* 1922. It had been opened in 1900 when the building was rented, but it was purchased in 1904 for £200. By 1923 it was decided to build new premises at a cost of £4,252 14*s*.

Carrville Co-op staff, 1924. Standing, left to right: Miss I.R. Scott, J.W. Ford, G. Coates, J.H. French, Miss W. Quinn. Seated: J. Kelly and W. Robinson.

The Mile Stone Inn, 106 High Street, Carrville, showing the landlord, J.C. Dunn, *c.* 1900. To the right of the door can be seen the milestone. In the 1850s it was known as the Two Mile Stone Inn. Now it is the site of Heron's Electrical Services.

An outing from The Grange Inn, Carrville, *c.* 1925. Seated on the far left is Mr Edward Cummings, blacksmith, from Malvern Terrace, Gilesgate. Standing on the left is Robert Gainforth.

Belmont Hall, 1932. Later, when it became a hotel, it reverted back to the name of its predecessor, Ramside Hall. Built by Thomas Pemberton when he purchased the estate for £13,000 in 1820, it incorporates part of the earlier house.

Dr John Stapylton Grey Pemberton of Belmont Hall, wearing the uniform of the High Sheriff for the County Palatine of Durham, 1930. He was also president of the Council of Durham Colleges. The photograph was taken by John Edis of Saddler Street.

Fitters and turners from the Grange Iron Works, Carrville, 1880s. The company had a huge export business trading to all parts of the world and was the largest company in the city. All kinds of heavy industrial machinery was made there: winding engines, steam engines, pumping engines, etc. It also had its own gas works which supplied the factory and offices.

William Dixon Slack at his lathe at the Grange Iron Works, Carrville, c. 1908 (see page 12). In May 1941 four bombs were dropped on the old iron works site which had been closed since 1926. Today the site near Maureen Terrace is occupied by a caravan park.

Office staff from the Grange Iron Works, Carrville, 1914–18. Back row: Evelyne Naisbett, Amy Curry, Maggie MacLennon, Mary Haswell, Laura Fenwick, Polly French, Flossy Gibbney, Ella Gibson. Front row: Elsie Foster, Mr Lacey, May Burn.

Miners from Carrville, c. 1910. Back row, left to right: -?-, Tommy Darling, Jack Britton, Ralph Miller, Kit Britton, Kit Richardson. Middle row: T. Carr, Tommy Russell, ? Russell, -?-, -?-. Front row: -?-. In the background is the old pit heap of the Grange Colliery, which stood near the Grange Iron Works.

The shop of John Tindale, butcher and farmer, Carrville, *c.* 1909. Old Mrs Tindale can be seen standing near the doorway, on the right. Mr Tindale had been killed on 4 February 1908 while ploughing in a field near Renny's Lane. Young John Tindale, his son, can be seen on the left outside the shop.

John Bagnall from Lowe the butcher (est. 1906), Carrville, April 1937. He was one of two boys chosen by the Belmont branch of the YMCA to represent them at the Coronation festivities in London. In time we may see the return of the butcher's bike!

CHAPTER FOUR

LOW & HIGH PITTINGTON
& HALLGARTH

PC Sidney Walton outside his police house, Low Pittington, c. 1913. The house was identified as a police house by the badge above the door. Sidney Walton had joined the Durham force in 1911 after serving in the Coldstream Guards. The young boy on the steps is Sidney Walton jnr.

Low Pittington, 1904. In the distance are the old limestone quarries which closed in about 1879. On the right is the old Institute building, now demolished, which was originally the school. The road in the distance leads to an area known locally as 'The Town' (see below).

Looking towards Broomside from the area of Low Pittington known as 'The Town', now the High Street, *c*. 1903. It is said to be the site of the original village. Centre right is Coronation Crescent, built in 1902 to mark the coronation of King Edward VII.

A Sunday outing from High Pittington, *c.* 1915. Front row: fourth from right, Nichol March; first on right, Tom March. Middle row: standing, third from right, Margaret Kellet, with Tom Kellet next to her, and behind them Annie Kellet. Standing third from the left is George William Hutchinson (see page 44).

Two policemen, thought to be at Pittington, *c.* 1910. Nichol March is on the left. Both carry the same number on their collar, 938. It is possible that Nichol was a special constable.

Pittington station, which was situated at Low Pittington on the Durham Elvet & Murton branch, *c.* 1910. On the right is the stationmaster, Mr Unwin; second from the right is George March, trainee porter/signalman (see page 4).

Pittington station, with a train from Sunderland, 1948. The G5 locomotives were regular performers on this line. The line opened in 1836 and the new station was authorised on 17 June 1875 at a cost of £383. The photograph was taken by C.W.A. Camwell.

The gates, Pittington station, *c.* 1910, showing the original North Eastern Railway signal-box which was demolished in 1938.

Pittington station, with Class J39 0–6–0, 64927 drawing a special train leaving for Durham Miners' Gala, 21 July 1951. The station closed to passengers on 3 January 1953 and to goods on 4 January 1960.

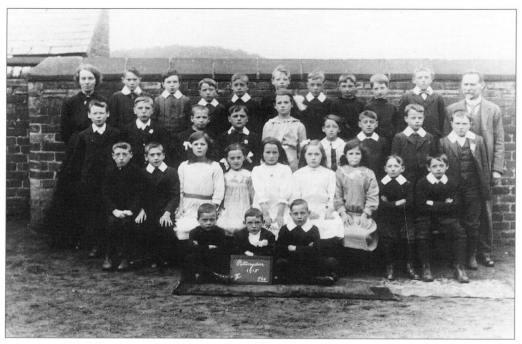

Class group from Low Pittington, 1915.

Football team from High Pittington school, 1922–3.

Pittington night-school group, 1870s. Back row, third from left, is James Clark, a founder member of the Pittington Co-operative Society. The class consisted of all ages from the village, eager to learn. At first the class was aimed just at children.

Tree planting at Low Pittington, Jubilee Day, May 1935. The planting of a number of Jubilee trees, the gift of Mrs W.W. Baker Baker of Elemore Hall (see page 54), was presided over by the Revd E.W. Bolland, under the auspices of the Garden Guild. The trees were planted by representatives of the Mothers' Union, the Salvation Army, unemployed persons, Garden Guild, Girls' Friendly Society, Girl Guides and the two Methodist churches. They were to mark the Silver Jubilee of King George V and Queen Mary. Afternoon tea was provided for the children.

The Duke of Wellington Inn, High Pittington, *c*. 1904. It is said to be named after the visit to Pittington by Lord Londonderry and the 'Iron Duke' himself in 1827. High Pittington was once known as New Pittington, and was built to accommodate miners and their families working at the 'Derry' (Londonderry) pit. The landlord, Mr Samuel T. Taylor, is standing in the left of the doorway, wearing a waistcoat.

Carnival parade outside the Duke of Wellington. The name 'Uncle Ned' is written on the reverse of the postcard. On the cart is seated an effigy of Kaiser Wilhelm, celebrating the end of the First World War. The chap holding the horse, dressed as Charlie Chaplin, is George William Hutchinson from Wellington Street (see page 48).

Pittington Co-op, founded 1874, *c*. 1924. This building was erected in 1897, and above the top window on the right is the inscription '1897 Diamond Jubilee', commemorating Queen Victoria's sixty years on the throne. The property is now split into three shops.

A horse-drawn van from Pittington Co-op (West Rainton Branch), an entrant for the Durham City Horse Parade, outside Vane Tempest Hall, Gilesgate, 1910. It has been said that a soldier was shot in the courtyard of the hall for mutiny, but official records have failed to confirm this. However, Sergeant-Major Smith shot himself at the barracks on 14 July 1911. He had served in India for twelve years, as well as in the South African War, 1899–1902. It is said that it is his ghost that haunts the barracks.

Fred Taylor of High Pittington proudly showing off his champion prize leeks, September 1955. Growing these vegetables was a popular pastime among the miners. The former agricultural village became a mining community when coal was discovered there in the early part of the nineteenth century, and it changed the whole aspect of village life. Row upon row of poor-quality cottages were built to house the miners, many of whom were newcomers to the area.

Pittington Co-op Leek Club, September 1953. Fred Taylor is holding his prize leeks, the best out of 118 stands. Fred spent all his working life as a miner, first at Elemore Colliery, then later at Sherburn Hill, where he was a deputy. Left to right: -?-, Billy Heslop, -?-, Arthur Mason, George Cummings, Fred Taylor, Jim Smith, -?-, -?-.

A group from Pittington seen prior to the annual trip to the seaside at Redcar, June 1950. Standing in the doorway at the back is Coun. the Revd A.W. Allen, vicar of St Lawrence's Church, Hallgarth. The building is the old Co-op shop which stood at the gable end of Glens Flats, now a private house.

High Pittington, showing The Duke of Wellington on the left, and on the right the miners' cottages in Wellington Street, c. 1904. The two boys are George William Hutchinson (on the left) and his brother James. During the great strike of 1844 which lasted nineteen weeks, Lord Londonderry, who owned many of the mines in the area, threatened to bring a workforce over from Ireland if his own men did not return to work. This he did, and today many descendants of these Irish still live in the village.

The old Bird in the Bush Inn (now demolished), which stood near Coalford Bridge, Coalford Lane, between High Pittington and Littletown, c. 1920. It became two houses in its final days. Immediately opposite, to the right, was a cockpit, where cock-fighting used to take place before it was outlawed in 1849.

Hallgarth Church, showing the clock tower and main entrance gates, *c.* 1916. The clock was installed in 1898 and dedicated in memory of Alfred Harrison of Old Pittington. The ornate lamp over the gates no longer exists and recently the porch doors and seats inside the porch have been removed.

An early engraving of Hallgarth Church seen from the south, before the restoration of 1846–7 by Ignatius Bonomi. The churchyard contains many fine memorials. One unusual plot is dedicated to the Baker Baker family of Elemore Hall, and consists of white marble crosses surrounded by metal railings.

Looking towards the chancel from the font. The sanctuary is seen boarded up, during its lengthening in 1905, when Canon S.B. Guest-Williams was vicar. To the left, on the north wall, is a memorial to James Barmby DD, Principal of Hatfield Hall 1859–76 and vicar of this church from 1875 to 1894. He died in Northallerton in 1897.

Looking towards the font, during the restoration of 1897–9. This is an unusual view without the pews. The architect was W.S. Hicks and the cost of the work carried out was more than £2,000. The columns on the right are Norman, *c.* 1170.

The font, photographed by Wilkinson of Durham
c. 1905. This font was given to the church by Dean
Waddington in 1847, who thought it 'unsuitable'
for Durham Cathedral. It was returned to the
cathedral in 1935 by Dean Alington. The old
Saxon font was sold and used as a cattle trough at
the Rift Farm, Pittington, and was brought back to
the church in the 1920s.

One of the Baker Baker memorials, Hallgarth
Church, c. 1913. It commemorates Ferdinand
Baker Baker of Elemore Hall (see page 54), who
died on 28 September 1909; also his sister,
Isabel Elizabeth Baker Baker, who died on
8 October 1911. Another sister's name was
added later, Eva Conyers Baker Baker, who died
on 2 March 1931.

The chancel, photographed in the 1950s by Eric Davies. It was entirely rebuilt early this century at a cost of £1,400, and extended 13 ft in the Early English style. It was therefore returned to the same length as the chancel that had been destroyed in 1848. The new chancel was dedicated, along with the new Harrison organ, by the Right Revd E.N. Hodges, Assistant Bishop of Durham, on 17 June 1905.

Hallgarth Mill, showing the Hugill (or Wakefield) family, 1920s. It was at this mill, on 8 August 1830, that Mary Ann Westrop was murdered by her fellow servant, George Clark. The original mill was built by the monks of Durham (who owned the manor of Pittington). It stood south of the church, near where the footbridge leading to Sherburn Village crosses the beck above the swampy ground.

CHAPTER FIVE

ELEMORE HALL & LITTLETOWN

Elemore Hall, c. 1905. The hall was originally a stone-built Elizabethan manor house, traces of which survive. The new house was built for George Baker in 1749–53 by architect and mason Robert Shout of Helmsley. The total cost after completion was about £3,000. The clock tower seen on the left still exists.

Elemore Hall in its former glory as a country mansion. In the 1950s it became a residential school for children with learning difficulties run by Durham County Council. Ann Isabella Milbanke, later to become the wife of poet Lord Byron, was born here in 1792.

Henry Conyers Baker Baker and the staff of Elemore Hall, 11 November 1933. This photograph shows the large number of staff which was needed to run an extensive country house. Descendants of the family now live at Sedbury Hall, near Richmond, North Yorkshire.

Gamekeepers on the Elemore Hall estate, *c.* 1905.

Spyall Cottage (an appropriate name for a gate-house), on the Elemore Hall estate, near Littletown, *c.* 1910. The cottage has now been demolished.

Littletown House, *c*. 1913. The home of the Hornsby family (see below), once the home of Thomas Crawford, mining manager and coal owner. Littletown was once called South Pittington, later Little Pittington and finally, in 1613, Littletown.

A member of the Hornsby family with chauffeur and car belonging to George Henry Hornsby, mining engineer, viewer and agent for Littletown and Sherburn Hill Colliery. The photograph was taken outside Littletown House in about 1913.

The Crossing, Littletown, *c.* 1910, showing the Duke of York public house, built in 1894, on the right, and in the centre, behind the roof-line, is the colliery headgear of Littletown Colliery (Lady Alice), which belonged to Lambton Collieries Ltd. It was sunk in 1834 and closed in 1913. Two famous men connected with this colliery were Peter Lee, who was a pony driver here, and John Wilson, the miners' leader.

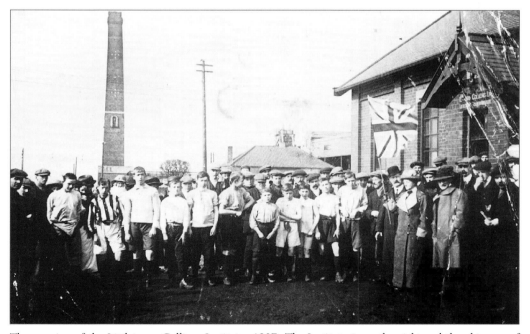

The opening of the Littletown Colliery Institute, 1907. The Institute is on the right and the chimney of the colliery on the left. The lady holding the flag is possibly a member of the Baker Baker family.

Miners' cottages, Pit Row, Littletown, 1910. Almost all mining villages had a street named Pit Row – the one nearest to, or leading to, the pit.

The Miners' Institute, Littletown, 1913. Above the door is written 'Lambton Collieries Ltd, Littletown Colliery Institute'. It was opened in 1907, with a well-equipped reading-room and two billiard tables. The building was demolished in the late 1970s.

Miners and families from Littletown, picking coal for heating and cooking from the old colliery pit heap, believed to be the 'Derry', during the miners' strike of May–November 1926.

Heather View, Littletown, showing miners' cottages shortly before they were demolished in the 1970s. Despite the pleasing name, they faced Sherburn Hill pit-heap (see page 63). This street stood to the right of the Duke of York public house.

Harvest festival, Littletown Wesleyan Chapel, *c.* 1908. The chapel was built in 1858 to seat 250 people at a cost of £300. After 121 years' service it closed in 1979. It is now a joiners' workshop.

Littletown Chapel group, outside the vestry door, 1920s. Back row, left to right: W. Shepherd, J. Fisk, W. Smith, Jack Watson, Charles Robinson, John Smith. Third row: Fred Robinson, Margery Shepherd, Jennie Blacklock, Edith Winn, Bella Lloyd, Jenny Shepherd, Nellie Lloyd, -?-. Second row: E. Robson, -?-, J. Blunt, Ed Sample. Front row: Maggie Gibson, Mary Cummings, -?-, Lizzie Blacklock, Mary Todd, G. Blunt and J. Fisk (in the wheelchair).

Littletown post office and Miss Annie Purvis, shopkeeper and sub-post-mistress, *c.* 1910. On the right can be seen the gable end of the Duke of York (now called Ramblers' Rest). This was issued as a Christmas postcard.

William Simpson, miner and bonesetter, Littletown, *c.* 1871. He was an interesting character who rode his horse wearing a distinctive top hat and swallow-tailed coat. A story about him is told in L. Moran's book on Brandon: A young putter was injured at the pit by a fall of stone. When he was brought to the surface two surgeons announced his legs were broken. They bandaged the legs up and added splints. For two days the boy suffered great pain. His father sent for Simpson, the bonesetter from Littletown. After removing the splints and bandages the boy was released from pain. Mr Simpson found that the legs were not broken and said that the boy could have died or been crippled for life if he had been left bandaged up. The Simpson family continued as bonesetters within living memory.

Class group, Littletown, 1915. In the second row on the right is William Shepherd. The school was built in 1874 for 200 children. The school logbook entry for 15 November 1915 gives mention of Richard Pretty, a young lad who had slid on the ice and broken his leg above the knee. He was immediately sent home where first aid was rendered by Mr Simpson, the bonesetter (see page 61). The school opened for the last time on 8 April 1960.

Littletown Cricket Club, August 1953, fourth from the top of the Durham Coast League. Back row, left to right: -?-, George Smith, Ron Meakin, Don Smith, Jack Squires, Jack Armstrong, Billy Tulip, Jack Simpson, Mr Meakin. Front row: Ned Cummings, Harry Rutter, Tom Meakin, Tom Goodchild, Alan Monroe. Centre front: Billy Simpson.

CHAPTER SIX

SHERBURN HILL

Sherburn Hill, looking down towards the 'Busty', showing the old pit heap, 1960s. This was one of the largest pit heaps in the county, covering 40 acres. Between 1969 and 1972 it was lowered from 583 ft to 440 ft at a cost of about £105,000. The area is now grassed and used as arable land.

Sherburn Hill Colliery, photographed by Billy Longstaff of Sherburn Village, 1950s. In the 1950s 938 men were employed, producing 7,600 tons of coal a week. The east shaft was commenced in 1830 and the west shaft in 1835. A surface-drift was started in 1951. The colliery closed in 1965.

James Turnbull Nairn, colliery engineer, Sherburn Hill, 1963. His claim to fame was that he held the record score of 34 for one over (five 6s and one 4), at Littletown cricket club (see page 62). He was the uncle of George Nairn of Chester-le-Street, a postcard collector.

Miners at the coal face, Sherburn Hill Colliery, with an Arc wall cutter in the five-quarter-seam, 1940. On 11 June 1948 four men were killed at the colliery by carbon monoxide poisoning after an explosion, which was caused by fire-damp.

The old colliery canteen, Sherburn Hill, January 1949. This photograph was used in the *Durham Advertiser* and was alongside a view of the new canteen then being built. The account said that the new canteen was to be one of the finest in the country.

Canteen group from Sherburn Hill during the miners' strike, May 1926. Back row, left to right: -?-, -?-, Bob Usher, -?-, (?) Jack Kyle, -?-, Arthur Dodd, -?-, -?-, (?) Billy Hewitson. The community banded together in an effort to feed all the children, and two meals a day were served in the Welfare Hall. The cooking was carried out by male cooks from the butchers' department of the Co-op (see page 68). Mr J. Huntley, headmaster of the boys' school, acted as secretary.

The opening of the pithead baths, Sherburn Hill Colliery, by Mr E.R.D. Skinner, Chairman of the Durham Division of the NCB, September 1950. Before this miners would go home black and bathe in the tin bath in front of the fire. The picture shows miners and their families. The young lad on the left of the front row is Fred Haywood. Mr Skinner remarked that the new baths were justified because the colliery could confidently look ahead fifty years before the coal supplies beneath would be exhausted. The pit closed fifteen years later, in July 1965.

Sherburn Hill miners' banner at the Big Meeting, July 1965. The banner is draped in black to signify the closing of the colliery that year. Pictured passing the Royal County Hotel, the banner depicts the Aged Miners' Homes at Sherburn Hill, opened in 1924.

Sherburn Hill Colliery Band, pictured outside the Miners' Welfare Hall at Sherburn Hill, July 1954. The bandmaster, third from the right in the front row, was Lumley Button (a relative of the author). Born at Dragonville, he moved to Sherburn Hill in 1911 and started work at Sherburn Hill pit at the age of thirteen; he spent forty-nine years working here. A member of the band for forty-eight years and bandmaster for twenty-one years, he died in 1968.

The Wesleyan Chapel, Sherburn Hill, *c.* 1910. Erected in 1857, the building was enlarged in 1884 to seat 313 people. It was used as an optical factory for many years and is now awaiting redevelopment as a private house.

The newly built Co-op building, Sherburn Hill, 1913. The first meeting of the society was held on 12 December 1873. Shortly after, in January 1874, the members were able to acquire the use of a colliery house, which they opened as a store. Three years later they had built up enough capital to build their own store; this was rebuilt in 1913, and is now a furniture store.

Horse-drawn greengrocer's cart from Sherburn Hill Co-op, 1920s. By 1919 'The Hill' had its own picture theatre (The Co-operative Picture Hall), now replaced by the primary schools.

Sherburn Hill Co-op's mobile shop, built by Fowler & Armstrong of Dragonville, 1950s. This was a welcome visitor to the local pit villages.

Front Street, Sherburn Hill, *c.* 1923. On the right is the old Londonderry Arms, now a private house. To the left of the pub are Albert Chapman, tailor, Florence Atkinson, grocer, the Seven Stars public house and Walter Willson's grocery shop.

Sherburn Hill branch of Walter Willson's grocery, *c.* 1924 (see above). Walter Willson opened his first shop at Bishop Auckland in 1875. The coming of the supermarket in the 1960s brought about a decline in the number of the firm's shops, which at one time reached 185. The business is now run by Edward Aitchison, a great-great-grandson of the founder.

Front Street, Sherburn Hill, *c.* 1900. On the left are the post office, the doctor's house and, set back, the 'Band Room', which was originally The National Girls' School, opened by the Revd R.G.L. Blenkinsop in 1845. On the right is the Wesleyan chapel (see page 68).

Sherburn Hill post office, *c.* 1910. Mr John Philipson, sub-postmaster, is in the doorway; he was also a grocer and draper. The window on the right displays picture postcards for sale. Today's post office is still on the same site.

The Miners' Welfare Hall and war memorial, Sherburn Hill, early 1930s. On the right of the Welfare is
Sherburn Hill Co-op store (see page 68) and, centre, the Aged Miners' Homes. The building to the right
of the far telegraph pole was Bennie Clark's shop (see opposite page).

Sherburn Hill Miners' Welfare Hall Committee, outside the Welfare Hall, 1926. Front row: third from
the left, John G.C. Huntley and, fifth from the left, Jack Kyle. The Welfare Hall was built in two stages,
the first being in 1926. In December that year a boot fund concert was held here to provide boots for
local schoolchildren. In 1929 an Institute was added at a cost of about £3,500; it was officially opened on
13 December 1929.

Matty Clark's, confectioners and cycle shop, Sherburn Hill, showing his son Bennie and his wife Minnie (the author's great uncle and aunt). Bennie later took over the shop from his father, Matthew, who had started as a confectioner in about 1925. Bennie later had a toy and cycle shop in Claypath, and also ran a stall in Durham Indoor Market, which had been started by his father.

James and Annie Button, c. 1911. They were parents of the bandmaster Lumley Button (see page 67). They moved to 25 Joicey Street, Sherburn Hill, from Dragonville in 1911 and they spent their final years living at the Aged Miners' Homes, Sherburn Hill. James was the brother of Edward (see page 2).

Looking down Sherburn Hill towards Sherburn, *c.* 1908. In the centre are the schools (see below). A dray can be seen delivering to the Oak Tree public house. On the right the children are standing outside the doctor's house.

The schools, Sherburn Hill, *c.* 1912. The cart is John Gustard's, fruit and potato merchant of Sherburn Hill. The school on the left is now two private residences. That on the right is now The Chimneys, a nursing home for the elderly.

Sherburn Hill United, winners of the Durham Amateur Challenge Cup, 1927. Back row, left to right: Tommy Kitching, -?-, Cecil Williamson, Geordie Smith, Jack Jenkins, Bobby McGibbon, -?-. Second row: -?-, -?-, -?-, Isaac Burrell, -?-, Bobby Goodchild, -?-, William Kitching, -?-, -?-, Albert Chapman, ? Hamilton. Front row: -?-, Tommy Kitching, -?-, -?-, Joe Jackson, -?-, George Lloyd, ? Prichard.

Sherburn Hill Boys, League Champions, 1923/4. Back row, left to right: Mr Chambers, J. Carroll, W. Johnson, S. Meredith, A. Stewart, W. Boal, W. Adair, Mr Huntley. Front row: H. Graham, W. Humes, A. Blanch (League Shield), G. Reveler (Capt.) (Samuelson Cup), W. Kay (Durham Shield), M. Local, S. Harrison.

Mrs Ena Armstrong, landlady of the Londonderry Arms (see page 70), Sherburn Hill, making a pan of prize broth, October 1958. See below for the end product.

Leek show members and customers enjoying a good old-fashioned pan of prize broth made by Mrs Ena Armstrong, October 1958. Left to right: Peter Gibbon, Tommy Ward, -?-, Pat Smith, Billy Pritchard, -?-. Back centre: Tommy Pritchard, Jack Pritchard, John Heaton, Billy Kenny.

CHAPTER SEVEN

SHADFORTH & LUDWORTH

Low View, Shadforth, looking west up the village from the bridge over the beck at the 'Bottom End', 1930s.
The building third on the right is the Saddle Inn, now a private house called The Old Saddle.

Shadforth, looking west up the village, *c.* 1926. The low building, to the left of the man who is standing, is the old post office. The left side of the photograph is shown in more detail below. The photograph was taken by Johnson of Gateshead.

Shadforth 'West End', *c.* 1920. The original has been marked: 'A, Village School; B & C, Farm Houses; and D, Village Green'.

John Carter (at the back) with his fruit and vegetable cart, seen near Shadforth post office, *c.* 1931. Matthew Cooper is at the front.

The South Durham Hunt, outside Dene House Farm, Shadforth, *c.* 1908. The hunt is still a familiar sight in the village. Two houses now occupy the site of the farmhouse. One of them has retained the name Dene House.

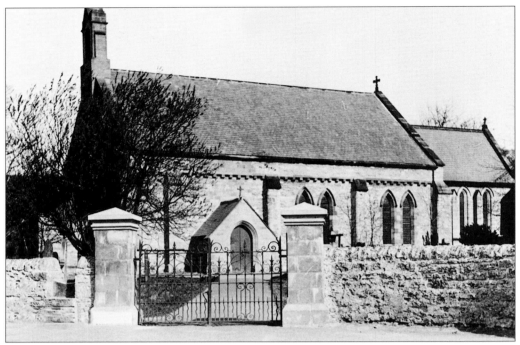

St Cuthbert's Church, Shadforth, *c.* 1923. It was consecrated by Bishop Maltby on 5 August 1839. The outside appearance today is rather poor, showing a mix of limestone with sandstone additions, badly weathered.

An interior view of St Cuthbert's Church, Shadforth, *c.* 1910. The photograph shows the old oil lamps which lit the church before the introduction of electricity.

Shadforth Mill, c. 1910. It was also known as Crawford's Mill after the last occupants. Robert Crawford was the son of Thomas Crawford of Littletown House (see page 56), who owned the mill. He worked the mill until his death in 1916. His widow continued to live at the mill until 1925, after which time it was deserted. It stood near Cold-knuckles Farm.

Cold-knuckles Farm, situated on the moors between Sherburn Hill and Running Waters, c. 1912. It was farmed by the Gilchrist family who still farm in the area. The last occupants were Lon and Betty Farley. It is now demolished, marked only by a pile of rubble and an overgrown garden.

Ludworth Tower, showing the west wall, which consists of three storeys over a vaulted basement, *c.* 1930. The surrounding village of Ludworth was originally in the possession of the de Ludworth family (*c.* 1210). In 1411 Bishop Langley leased the manor of Ludworth to Thomas Holden for life. The tower formed part of a larger manor house which was fortified by Thomas Holden in 1422 by licence of Bishop Langley. A considerable part of the tower fell in February 1890. The ruin is now looked after by Durham City Council.

Ludworth miners, 1924. The original photograph is titled 'The Boys', and shows the staff involved in the re-sinking of Ludworth shaft from the main coal seam in Low Hutton seam. Back row, left to right: enginewright, office clerk, winding engineman, sinker, sinker, pump fitter, sinker. Front row: banksman, pump fitter, banksman, banksman, banksman, sinker.

CHAPTER EIGHT

SHERBURN VILLAGE

St Mary's Church, Sherburn Village, c. 1913. The church was consecrated on 28 May 1872 by the Right Revd Charles Baring, Lord Bishop of Durham. The architect was Austin & Johnson of Newcastle, and the builder Robson & Son of Durham. The total cost was about £3,400 of which £1,800 was given by Mr C.T. Thompson of Ashdown Park, Sussex, and of Sherburn Hall. In 1874 the Harrison organ was installed.

Front Street, Sherburn Village, *c.* 1906. On the right is the old church school, opened in 1804 by Arthur Mowbray and rebuilt by Mrs Pemberton of Sherburn Hall in 1848, at a cost of £640. It closed as a school in 1913, when the new council school opened (see page 91).

The crossroads, Sherburn Village, 1913. The horse and cart are standing outside Wilkinson's shop, now Gatenby's. The two properties in the centre of the photograph no longer exist. The building on the far right was the old reading-room, now retail premises.

The village green, Sherburn, *c.* 1900. The green is owned by the Church Commissioners. In 1897, to celebrate Queen Victoria's Diamond Jubilee, a line of trees was planted; some can be seen to the right. The idea of tree-planting continued at Sherburn for the coronations of George V, VI and Elizabeth II.

The crossroads looking towards Durham. On the right is the Lambton Arms where, on 1 May 1868, PC John Cruickshank was shot by his fellow officer, David Paton, after which Paton shot himself outside the pub. The *Durham County Advertiser* gave a full account of the story. Cruickshank's headstone can be seen in Hallgarth churchyard, Pittington.

The white-washed coachyard buildings belonging to Sherburn Hall, 1950s. They are now demolished, and on the site is the steward's bungalow belonging to Sherburn Village Working Men's Club, part of which can be seen on the right.

Sherburn Hall, a grand gentleman's house for such a small village. It has been lived in by several well-known Durham families: the Tempests of Old Durham, the Pembertons, T.C. Thompson, MP, Coulson the pit-sinker, Nelson the builder and others. The last occupant was Dr Harrison, who saw his patients in rooms on the ground floor. The Hall became the property of Durham Rural District Council and was used for civil defence activities during the Second World War. It was demolished in about 1952. The photograph was taken by Dr C.W. Gibby.

Sherburn House Welfare, Sherburn Village, opened in 1929 for Sherburn House Colliery. After Sherburn House closed in 1931 it was taken over by the Welfare Commission. In 1952 Sherburn Hill took it over until it finally closed in 1965. It fell into disuse and after some time it was destroyed in a fire on 28 March 1967. It stood near the present bowling green. The photograph was taken by Ray Kitchen.

A winter shooting party from Sherburn, *c.* 1912. Left to right: William Smithson, miner (with Caesar the dog), Peter Oswald, farmer, Craig Simpson, publican, Mr Parkin, of Sherburn Hill, Mr Rutherford, land agent.

Sherburn Aged Miners' Homes shortly before they were officially opened, *c.* 1913. They were named the George Parkinson Memorial Homes in memory of a local Methodist preacher, author of *True Stories of Durham Pit Life*. The land was given by Lord Joicey, via the Lambton Hetton & Joicey Company.

The visit to Sherburn Aged Miners' Homes by Susan Lawrence MP, Under Secretary to the Minister of Health, 17 January 1930. She is accompanied by the President of the Association, Mr W. Whitely and Vice-President Alderman J. Gilliland; she visited some of the miners' homes in the Durham area. The picture shows William Scott Harper and his wife Martha standing on their step.

Sherburn Colliery station from the Belmont side, *c.* 1915. The bridge is the one which you pass on entering Sherburn from Durham. The building on the right is now demolished and the site is occupied by an allotment garden.

The north side of Sherburn Colliery station, 1950s. On the right is the old colliery headgear of the Lady Durham Pit, sunk on 7 October 1873.

Officers of 1st Sherburn Scout Troop, *c.* 1910. One former member believed to be in this group was Dr Alex Harrison, who became the village doctor.

Assembling gas masks at Sherburn Village, 29 September 1938. In the centre is Mrs L. Roberts and Tommy Nicholson is on the right. This photograph was printed in the *Durham County Advertiser* under the heading 'Air raid precautions speed up in County Durham', one year before the war was declared. The photograph was taken inside Sherburn Hall, which was taken over by Durham County Council as HQ for defence activities.

Sherburn County Council Mixed Primary School, 1913. It was opened by Mr J.L. Parkinson on 14 February of that year, and had been built at a cost of £5,446 16s 10d. The school having been demolished the site is now occupied by School Court, comprising elderly people's bungalows.

A group photograph from Sherburn Council School, Form III, 1920. Back row, left to right: Rowley Welsh, -?-, Jacky Irwin, Lesley Cooper, Jack Davis, -?-, ? Watson, Martin Tate. Middle row: Gertie Wardrobe, Elsie Carr, ? Ryans, Mary Alice Harper, Nellie Atkinson, -?-, Mary Simpson, Ena Wardrobe, Ada Smithson, (?) teacher. Front row: Arthur Davis, Edith Smithson, Bessie Ayre, Marjorie Irwin, Nellie Irwin, ? Cooper, Molly Cooper, -?-, Jenny Smithson.

Sherburn Village Co-op, 1920s. It was opened as a branch of the Sherburn Hill Co-op store in 1899, and it is now Sherburn Village Community Centre.

The Old Mill, Sherburn (also known as Sherburn House Mill), which stood to the south of the crossroads looking towards Grand View, c. 1920. By 1940 it was not listed on any map, so is thought to have been demolished in the mid-1930s.

CHAPTER NINE

SHERBURN HOUSE (HOSPITAL)

The Revd Henry Arthur Mitton MA, Master of Sherburn House from 1874 to 1913, seen with his four daughters at Sherburn Hospital. Left to right: Rosa Sanders, Evelyn Maynard, Nan Baker and 'Jems'. The photograph was taken by George Fillingham in about 1912.

Sherburn House Hospital gateway, 1907. Though much altered in about 1896, it still retains its fourteenth-century vaulted arch. Poor travellers were given food at the gate well into the eighteenth century. Opposite the gateway is an interesting churchyard belonging to Sherburn House. One of the memorials is to Thomas Simpson, who died on 10 July 1877, and was a brother of the hospital from 1869 to 1877. It records that he was in the 23rd Royal Welsh Fusiliers and was present throughout the Battle of Waterloo (1815).

The main hospital building, 1930s. The hospital was founded in about 1183 by Hugh Le Puiset, Bishop of Durham, as a leper hospital. In 1434 the hospital was reorganised to provide for thirteen poor men and also two lepers, 'if they can be found', clear evidence that leprosy had declined. The infirmary, the new hospital with facilities for the treatment of thirty patients, was built in 1864 at a cost of £14,000 by Austin & Johnson, but was not opened for patients until 1872.

The fire of 27 April 1912 which destroyed most of the north wing of the hospital. The extension was only two years old, and about £2,000-worth of damage was caused. The fire was discovered by Miss Fair, the brethren's cook, at about 6.30 pm. The hospital brigade (Mr G. Davison and others) were joined by Durham City Brigade at 8 pm. Finally Durham and Northumberland Collieries Fire and Rescue Brigade arrived at 9 pm.

Fire damage in one of the corridors. Staff and patients who could not return to their homes were taken to the dispensary where beds were made up (see page 96). Hundreds of people from nearby villages gathered to watch. The fire was described in the *Durham Advertiser* as 'burning like a roaring furnace'.

The dispensary, Sherburn House, *c.* 1900. The first dispensary, giving free 'out-patient' treatment for the poor of the area, had opened in 1858. This new detached dispensary opened in 1883 (the date is on the stained glass window in the left bay). It was designed in the Tudor style by C. Hodgson Fowler at a cost of about £2,000.

The church in the hospital grounds, 1930s. It was built shortly after the hospital was founded for the maintenance of sixty-five poor lepers. It was damaged by fire in 1850 and again in 1859, when it was restored by Austin of Newcastle at a cost of about £2,000. All of this restoration was destroyed in the fire of 4 December 1864 (the *Durham County Advertiser*, 9 December 1864). After standing derelict for four years it was restored in 1868. In the sanctuary floor there is a plaque inscribed: 'Thomas Leaver Preacher to King Edward the Sixte, He died in July 1577.'

The Master's house, built 1832, seen here in the 1930s. The armorial bearings over the porch are those of the Revd G.S. Faber, who was Master from 1832 to 1854, and of Van Mildert, who was Bishop of Durham at the time of the rebuilding.

The Brethren's quarters, Sherburn Hospital, 1930s. The quarters were built in 1760 and consisted of two rooms per brother with adjacent communal dining hall. It is now called Thornley House after the hospital's long connection with the Manor of Thornley.

Hospital staff, *c.* 1913. Seated, left to right: McGuire, the gasman, Scarr, the messenger, Chapman snr, gardener and handyman. Standing: Albert, son of Michael (?), the estate carpenter, Henry Brown, J. Dixon, tree felling, etc., Joseph Bramley, carter, and G. Davidson, the gardener.

Mr Davidson, the hospital gardener, in the walled garden, 1910. Many daffodils are planted in the grounds and a pleasant walk, behind the hospital, takes its name ('the golden mile') from them. An open day in spring called Daffodil Sunday gives the public the opportunity of coming to see them.

Mr and Mrs Chapman with cows Nancy, Dolly and the calf, *c.* 1910.

Staff and patients of the hospital, October 1913. Joan Rose is sitting on 'sister's knee' on the right of the photograph. In 1925 the hospital was recognised as a training school, and tonsil and adenoid cases were undertaken for Durham County Council 'by contract'.

Sherburn House station, photographed by George Fillingham, *c.* 1914. In 1914 nine west-bound and eight east-bound trains were using the station daily, with an additional east-bound train on Saturday afternoons. The station closed for passenger traffic at the same time as Elvet in 1931. An exception was made for Miners' Gala specials and this privilege continued until 1953.

Harry Spraggon, stationmaster at Sherburn House, *c.* 1927. Harry had put in fifty-four years at Sherburn House, starting as a telegraph boy and later taking over from his father as stationmaster.

CHAPTER TEN

BOWBURN

*Bowburn banner at the Miners' Gala, seen on the
racecourse, early 1950s. The banner carried the
inscriptions 'You have nothing to lose but your chains'
and 'United to obtain the just reward of our labour'.*

St John's Mission, Bowburn, was built in about 1926 and is seen here in the 1930s. Mr Grainger, a haulage contractor, converted the church into a bungalow called Ravenswood in March 1967. On the left is the Hare and Greyhound (originally the Hare and Hounds).

Looking through Bowburn from Durham, 1909. In the centre is Durham Road, which was the first street of colliery houses and was built in 1910. On the right is Durham Road West, below which was built the Wesleyan chapel, which was opened in February 1910 by Lady Bell.

Bowburn post office, with the name D. Cook above the window, *c*. 1909. It is now Hill Rise guest house. The shop in the centre was Schellenberg's butcher's shop, now Bowburn Chop Suey House.

Members of Bowburn Women's Institute celebrating their twenty-fifth anniversary on 14 October 1949. They were formed on 21 October 1924 but the Institute was sadly suspended on 3 November 1987. The WI now has 112 branches in County Durham.

Bowburn School, 14 November 1913. The school was opened in August 1909 on land given by the colliery owners Bell Brothers. The railings surrounding the school were taken down to provide iron for the war effort during the Second World War.

The Pit Laddie, Bowburn, *c.* 1924. It stood near to the Bowburn interchange on the Durham to Coxoe Road. It was demolished to make way for the A1(M) in the 1960s.

Bowburn Albion football team, 1910/11. Middle row: Bill Whitman, -?-, Jack Willey.

Bowburn football team, photographed by Chisholm of Coxhoe, 1930/1. Back row, left to right: Frankie Morris, Tommy Jordan, Charlie Bainbridge, Arthur Thompson, Tommy Moore, Mr Haigh (rear), Ralph Kirkup, Jack Welsh, Jim Scott, J. Swinbanks (rear), Reuben Spence, Sid Smith, Bob Pattinson (rear), Ikey Smalley. Front row: -?-, Harold Alderson, Curle brothers from Ferryhill, ? Davison, -?-, George Scott, Harry Bell.

Bowburn Colliery, owned by Bell Brothers Ltd, 1911. It was the second to bear the name (the first, a small affair, was sunk in 1840 and abandoned in 1857). On 23 July 1906 the ceremonial cutting of the turf was done by the daughter of Sir Hugh Bell. The first coals were mined in October 1908 when coal-hewers were paid 1s 2½d per ton. Sunk to relieve heavy haulage at Tursdale, Bowburn closed in July 1967 (see page 101 for banner). When the pit first started producing coal 100 men were employed with an output of 600 tons a day. The average weekly wage for a face-worker was 26s per week, with free coal and a house.

Bowburn Colliery emergency staff and maintenance men during the 1926 miners' strike (May to November). During the 1926 strike many miners and their families travelled to the old Shincliffe Colliery pit-heap to pick coal to provide a fire for cooking. The author's grandfather, Jimmy Savage, spent most of his working life at Bowburn Colliery as a 'banksman'.

BOWBURN COLLIERY RACES.
Wednesday, May 4th, 1921.
For Pit Ponies Ridden Bare-back by Pit-Boys, with Pit-Bridles & Reins.

JUDGES:- Messrs M.R.Kirby, Esq. & P.Harle, Esq

STEWARDS; Messrs Barkhouse, Chitby, Hepple, Galley, Iseton, R.Ramsay, Elliot, Chapman & Sowerby.

Handicapper & Clerk of the Course, W.F.Gardner.

FIRST RACE 2 P.M.
Admission to Field 3d. Race Cards 3d.

PROCEEDS for the VILLAGE RELIEF FUND.

A poster advertising Bowburn Races, 4 May 1921, which were held during the miners' strike of 1921, 'The Great Lock Out' (1 April to 1 July). The races were held on 'The Bogs', which was west of the colliery.

Bowburn Races, 1921. These were for pit ponies (in the County of Durham) that had worked in the mine for at least three months prior to 31 March 1921. The rules stated: 'To be ridden by pit lads, bare back, with pit bridles and reins.'

Bowburn miners, *c.* 1908. Many of the first miners were brought from Page Green Colliery near Spennymoor, which was being closed around the time Bowburn was sunk.

Tursdale miners, 10 July 1905. Tursdale Pit was sunk in 1859–60 and was later linked up with Bowburn. The site was opened as a training centre for mine-workers on 28 July 1956. With the closing of the Durham Coal Field it is now Tursdale Engineering Ltd.

CHAPTER ELEVEN

HIGH SHINCLIFFE

Mr and Mrs J.G. Willis outside High Shincliffe post office and grocers, which they ran, c. 1910. High Shincliffe came about because of the opening of Shincliffe colliery in 1837. It was situated at the top of Shincliffe Bank and so was commonly known as Bank Top Colliery. It was abandoned in 1886.

The visit of Queen Mary to the Aged Miners' Homes at High Shincliffe, 26 November 1913. She arrived at 1 o'clock, with Mr John Wilson MP. She is seen entering the home of Mr and Mrs Patrick Millward, Dean Ede Street. She was staying at Lambton Castle for a week, the guest of Lord Durham.

Mr James Hall, a veteran of the Crimean War, sitting outside 5 Bishop Wescott Street, his Aged Miners' Home, at High Shincliffe, 26 November 1913. During the visit of Queen Mary (see above) he stood to attention on her arrival and later had the opportunity to talk to Her Majesty. He had been nominated for one of the houses by Urpeth Busty Lodge. He moved into his house in January 1903 after twenty-six years' service at the Birtley Iron Co. The site of the Aged Miners' Homes (which consisted of sixty-four miners' cottages) was purchased on 10 December 1901 from Mr J.A. Love for £300.

Jubilee tree-planting, May 1935. This was organised by the Silver Jubilee Committee appointed by Shincliffe Parish Council. Mr J.G. Willis is seen having just planted the tree near Shincliffe Bank top chapel.

Another tree was planted in the village after a service in the church. Mr C. Brooke is seen having just planted it on the Village Green, Jubilee Day, May 1935. Members of the Brooke family were market gardeners in the village. They now own Shincliffe Mill Nursery.

The Oak Tree public house, High Shincliffe (landlord John Mallan), *c.* 1900. High Shincliffe was then also known as Bank Top. The post office and grocers can be seen on the far left.

Mr J.G. Willis outside the post office and grocers at High Shincliffe, proudly showing off his new van in the 1920s. In Kelly's Directory of 1902 the premises were listed as a salt and whiting dealer as well as a post office.

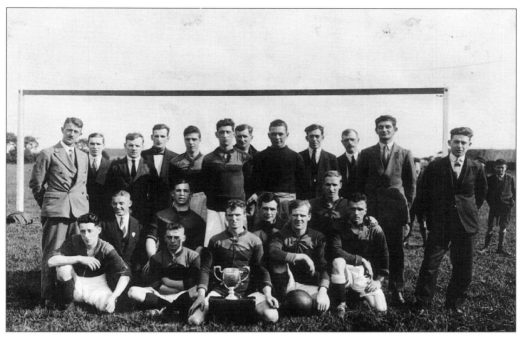

Shincliffe football team, late 1920s. Standing on the left is Mr H. Appleton, teacher at Shincliffe School. A large number of Bowburn miners lived at High Shincliffe.

A school group from Shincliffe, *c.* 1927. In the centre of the back row is Norman Wilson. Front row, left to right: -?-, Daisy Heaton, Edith Robson and Helen Blackett. The teachers are Miss Gallifant and Mr H. Appleton.

Shincliffe station from a postcard, *c.* 1910. The old signal cabin no longer exists. However, the old station is now a thriving restaurant.

Shincliffe station, 1950s. It was opened in 1844 by the North Eastern Railway. The new line linked Ferryhill to Leamside.

CHAPTER TWELVE

SHINCLIFFE VILLAGE

Shincliffe Village, looking towards High Shincliffe, c. 1900. On the left, the cottage with small upper windows was later heightened. It is now known as The Cottage.

St Mary's Church, Shincliffe Village, *c.* 1910, consecrated by Bishop Maltby on St Oswald's Day, 5 August 1851. The spire was added as a testimonial to the Revd Isaac Todd by parishioners and friends in 1871. The churchyard contains many interesting memorials; for example, William Martin, a blacksmith of Shincliffe Colliery who lost his life in an accident at Houghall Pit on 8 February 1872.

Inside St Mary's Church, *c.* 1910. Begun in 1850, it was designed by George Pickering, Clerk of Works at Durham Cathedral, at a cost of £1,600. A fire on 4 August 1980, which was deliberately started, caused some damage although it was not too serious.

Shincliffe Village, seen from the direction of Durham, *c.* 1905. In the centre, above the old railway embankment, can be seen the spire of St Mary's Church. To the left is the road leading to the Back Lane (see below), which became the village bypass in 1934.

The Back Lane, *c.* 1910. On the morning of Christmas Day 1924 a resident of old Durham was on his way to work via the lane when he saw a ghostly figure emerge from the darkness in the churchyard and then suddenly disappear. It was believed to have been the ghost of Mrs Noble, the wife of the miller at Shincliffe Mill, who was murdered on 22 August 1597. She is said to walk from the village to Sherburn hospital.

Shincliffe Village post office, 1924. In 1780 John Wesley preached to a large crowd in Shincliffe Village from the steps of the Manor House (see page 121).

Shincliffe Village post office and grocers, with Mrs Alice Mason on the left, *c.* 1910. It is now a private house called The Old Post Office.

Lambing time at Shincliffe with Fred Darnton, farm-hand working at Manor Farm, January 1936.

The Palmer family of Shincliffe Village, *c.* 1910. Back row, left to right: Constance, Robert (father), Margaret; middle row: Robert (junior); front row: William, James, Mary, Mary (mother) and Maud. Robert (senior) was a painter and decorator by trade; William died while serving in the navy and was buried in Egypt; Robert (junior) was a miner at Sherburn Hill; and James was a teacher at Shotton Colliery.

Harry Peele's shoeing and general smiths, Shincliffe Village, c. 1915. It stood to the left of the church hall and is now a private house called Forge Cottage. Lily Featherstone is seen standing in the doorway. Her father, Charles Wesley Featherstone, is on the far right of the photograph. The letters RSS stand for Registered Shoeing Smith.

High Street, Shincliffe Village, c. 1910. Loosely described as the village of the academics, few if any of the original families live there today.

Shincliffe Village Wesleyan Methodist chapel on the right, 1920s. It was built in 1874 to seat a congregation of 125, at a cost of £453. On the left is the parish hall belonging to St Mary's Church.

The Old Manor House, Shincliffe Village, 1905. It was also known as Manor Farm and was one of the smaller farms in the village. It lost its out-buildings when the new houses of Manor Close were erected.

The Seven Stars public house (centre), Shincliffe Village, 1920s. A cart is on its way up the steep hill to High Shincliffe.

An engraving of Whitwell Colliery by T.H. Hair, c. 1840. It stood between High Shincliffe and Sherburn House, near to Whitwell House. In 1836 'A' pit was sunk, and 'B' pit in 1840.

CHAPTER THIRTEEN

HOUGHALL

Milkmaids at Durham County Council's Farm, Houghall, carrying their stools and pails, December 1937.

Laying of the foundation stone at Houghall College, by C. Nathan, Assistant Secretary of the Ministry of Agriculture, 7 July 1937. The stone is to the left of the main entrance. The college was officially opened on 20 October 1938 by the Rt Hon. William Shepherd Morrison, MC, KC, MP, Minister of Agriculture and Fisheries.

An aerial view of Houghall College, late 1940s. It was designed by William Carter, ARIBA, and built by Durham County Council at a cost of about £60,000. The contractor was Mr Pearson.

A rare view of Houghall Manor House, 1930s. It was a sixteenth- or early seventeenth-century moated manor house. It had been much altered, but still contained many interesting features such as a secret chamber in the main chimney, a fine Tudor fireplace and a Jacobean well-staircase. It is said that Oliver Cromwell stayed here when passing through Durham, a guest of Sir Arthur Haselrig. It was demolished by 1964. Behind the house can be seen Cross Street (see below), the pit heap from Houghall Colliery and, top right, Durham Water Works (see page 126).

Cross Street, Houghall, 1920s. In its final years it became a colony of aged miners, and is now part of Houghall nature trail. The miners' cottages were built in about 1860 for Houghall Colliery, which was sunk in 1840.

Durham Water Works, 1930s. The plant stood to the left of Shincliffe Bridge on the Durham side. It was started by a private company which was registered in 1847 and started to supply water to the city in 1849. The water was pumped from the river Wear to filtering beds and then to a tank, finally being pumped to a service reservoir at Mountjoy. In about 1880 it was amalgamated with the Weardale and Shildon District Water Company.

The Aged Miners' Institute, Houghall, built in the early 1930s by Durham County Miners' Welfare Scheme.

The remains of the old Fever Hospital at Houghall shortly before it was demolished in about 1956. It was well established as an infectious disease hospital by 1897.

Members of the Land Army at Houghall, October 1940. They are seen prior to being entertained to tea by the County Committee on the occasion of presentations of good service badges. After visiting the cinema in the afternoon the girls proceeded to Lyons Café, Silver Street, where the presentations took place.

The author, Michael Richardson.

ACKNOWLEDGEMENTS

So many people have donated photographs that it is impossible to thank them all individually. Without their help this book would not have been possible. Special thanks go to my wife Norma, Miss D.M. Meade, Prof. G.R. Batho, Mrs H. Batho, Ray Kitching, Wilf Dodd, George Nairn, J. Lightly, J. Gosden, D. Wilcock, B. Hall and the late Mrs J. Adamson.

Staff of the following institutions have helped in various ways: The History of Education Project at Durham University, Palace Green Library, Durham City Reference Library, Durham Record Office, Beamish Museum and Durham Heritage Centre and Museum (North Bailey).

If any readers have new material or information they should contact Michael Richardson, 128 Gilesgate, Durham, DH1 1QG. Tel. 0191 3841427.